This Book Belongs to

Species	Weight	Size	Time

DATE	**WEATHER CONDITIONS**
TIME	
LOCATION	
COORDINATES	**WATER VISIBILITY**
FISHING PARTNER	CLEAR 1 2 3 4 5 MISTY
GEAR & EQUIPMENT	**MOON PHASE**
FISH BAIT & LURES	**BODY OF WATER**
	☐ LAKE ☐ RIVER ☐ CANAL
	☐ SEA ☐ OCEAN ☐ OTHER

NOTES

Species	Weight	Size	Time

DATE

TIME

LOCATION

COORDINATES

FISHING PARTNER

GEAR & EQUIPMENT

FISH BAIT & LURES

WEATHER CONDITIONS

WATER VISIBILITY

CLEAR 1 2 3 4 5 MISTY

MOON PHASE

BODY OF WATER

☐ LAKE	☐ RIVER	☐ CANAL
☐ SEA	☐ OCEAN	☐ OTHER

NOTES

Species	Weight	Size	Time

DATE	

TIME	

LOCATION	

COORDINATES	

FISHING PARTNER	

GEAR & EQUIPMENT

FISH BAIT & LURES

WEATHER CONDITIONS

WATER VISIBILITY

CLEAR 1 2 3 4 5 MISTY

MOON PHASE

BODY OF WATER

- [ ] LAKE
- [ ] RIVER
- [ ] CANAL
- [ ] SEA
- [ ] OCEAN
- [ ] OTHER

NOTES

Species	Weight	Size	Time

DATE

TIME

LOCATION

COORDINATES

FISHING PARTNER

GEAR & EQUIPMENT

FISH BAIT & LURES

WEATHER CONDITIONS

WATER VISIBILITY

| CLEAR | 1 | 2 | 3 | 4 | 5 | MISTY |

MOON PHASE

BODY OF WATER

| ☐ LAKE | ☐ RIVER | ☐ CANAL |
| ☐ SEA | ☐ OCEAN | ☐ OTHER |

NOTES

Species	Weight	Size	Time

DATE	
TIME	
LOCATION	
COORDINATES	
FISHING PARTNER	

GEAR & EQUIPMENT

FISH BAIT & LURES

WEATHER CONDITIONS

WATER VISIBILITY

1 2 3 4 5
CLEAR — MISTY

MOON PHASE

BODY OF WATER

- [ ] LAKE
- [ ] RIVER
- [ ] CANAL
- [ ] SEA
- [ ] OCEAN
- [ ] OTHER

NOTES

Species	Weight	Size	Time

DATE	

TIME	

LOCATION	

COORDINATES	

FISHING PARTNER	

GEAR & EQUIPMENT

FISH BAIT & LURES

WEATHER CONDITIONS

WATER VISIBILITY

CLEAR 1 2 3 4 5 MISTY

MOON PHASE

BODY OF WATER

☐ LAKE	☐ RIVER	☐ CANAL
☐ SEA	☐ OCEAN	☐ OTHER

NOTES

Species	Weight	Size	Time

DATE

TIME

LOCATION

COORDINATES

FISHING PARTNER

GEAR & EQUIPMENT

FISH BAIT & LURES

WEATHER CONDITIONS

WATER VISIBILITY

CLEAR 1 2 3 4 5 MISTY

MOON PHASE

BODY OF WATER

| ☐ LAKE | ☐ RIVER | ☐ CANAL |
| ☐ SEA | ☐ OCEAN | ☐ OTHER |

NOTES

Species	Weight	Size	Time

DATE

TIME

LOCATION

COORDINATES

FISHING PARTNER

GEAR & EQUIPMENT

FISH BAIT & LURES

WEATHER CONDITIONS

WATER VISIBILITY

CLEAR 1 2 3 4 5 MISTY

MOON PHASE

BODY OF WATER

☐ LAKE	☐ RIVER	☐ CANAL
☐ SEA	☐ OCEAN	☐ OTHER

NOTES

Species	Weight	Size	Time

DATE	WEATHER CONDITIONS
TIME	☀ ⛅ 🌧 ⛈ ❄
LOCATION	
COORDINATES	WATER VISIBILITY
FISHING PARTNER	CLEAR 1 2 3 4 5 MISTY

GEAR & EQUIPMENT

MOON PHASE

FISH BAIT & LURES

BODY OF WATER		
☐ LAKE	☐ RIVER	☐ CANAL
☐ SEA	☐ OCEAN	☐ OTHER

NOTES

Species	Weight	Size	Time

DATE

TIME

LOCATION

COORDINATES

FISHING PARTNER

GEAR & EQUIPMENT

FISH BAIT & LURES

WEATHER CONDITIONS

WATER VISIBILITY

CLEAR 1 2 3 4 5 MISTY

MOON PHASE

BODY OF WATER

☐ LAKE	☐ RIVER	☐ CANAL
☐ SEA	☐ OCEAN	☐ OTHER

NOTES

Species	Weight	Size	Time

DATE	
TIME	
LOCATION	
COORDINATES	
FISHING PARTNER	

GEAR & EQUIPMENT

FISH BAIT & LURES

WEATHER CONDITIONS

WATER VISIBILITY

CLEAR 1 2 3 4 5 MISTY

MOON PHASE

BODY OF WATER

- [ ] LAKE
- [ ] RIVER
- [ ] CANAL
- [ ] SEA
- [ ] OCEAN
- [ ] OTHER

NOTES

Species	Weight	Size	Time

DATE

TIME

LOCATION

COORDINATES

FISHING PARTNER

GEAR & EQUIPMENT

FISH BAIT & LURES

WEATHER CONDITIONS

WATER VISIBILITY

CLEAR 1 2 3 4 5 MISTY

MOON PHASE

BODY OF WATER

☐ LAKE	☐ RIVER	☐ CANAL
☐ SEA	☐ OCEAN	☐ OTHER

NOTES

Species	Weight	Size	Time

DATE	
TIME	
LOCATION	
COORDINATES	
FISHING PARTNER	

GEAR & EQUIPMENT

FISH BAIT & LURES

WEATHER CONDITIONS

WATER VISIBILITY

CLEAR 1 2 3 4 5 MISTY

MOON PHASE

BODY OF WATER

- [ ] LAKE
- [ ] RIVER
- [ ] CANAL
- [ ] SEA
- [ ] OCEAN
- [ ] OTHER

NOTES

Species	Weight	Size	Time

DATE	WEATHER CONDITIONS

TIME

LOCATION

COORDINATES

WATER VISIBILITY

CLEAR 1 2 3 4 5 MISTY

FISHING PARTNER

GEAR & EQUIPMENT

MOON PHASE

FISH BAIT & LURES

BODY OF WATER

- [ ] LAKE
- [ ] RIVER
- [ ] CANAL
- [ ] SEA
- [ ] OCEAN
- [ ] OTHER

NOTES

Species	Weight	Size	Time

DATE	
TIME	
LOCATION	
COORDINATES	
FISHING PARTNER	

GEAR & EQUIPMENT

FISH BAIT & LURES

WEATHER CONDITIONS

WATER VISIBILITY

CLEAR 1 2 3 4 5 MISTY

MOON PHASE

BODY OF WATER

- [ ] LAKE
- [ ] RIVER
- [ ] CANAL
- [ ] SEA
- [ ] OCEAN
- [ ] OTHER

NOTES

Species	Weight	Size	Time

DATE	
TIME	
LOCATION	
COORDINATES	
FISHING PARTNER	

GEAR & EQUIPMENT

FISH BAIT & LURES

WEATHER CONDITIONS

🌡 ___ ☀ ⛅ ☁ ⛈ ❄

🚩 ___ ☐ ☐ ☐ ☐ ☐

WATER VISIBILITY

☀ 1 — 2 — 3 — 4 — 5 ☁
CLEAR ○ ○ ○ ○ ○ MISTY

MOON PHASE

● ● ◐ ☾ ○
☐ ☐ ☐ ☐ ☐

BODY OF WATER

☐ LAKE	☐ RIVER	☐ CANAL
☐ SEA	☐ OCEAN	☐ OTHER

NOTES

Species	Weight	Size	Time

DATE	

TIME	

LOCATION	

COORDINATES	

FISHING PARTNER	

GEAR & EQUIPMENT

FISH BAIT & LURES

WEATHER CONDITIONS

WATER VISIBILITY

CLEAR 1 2 3 4 5 MISTY

MOON PHASE

BODY OF WATER

☐ LAKE	☐ RIVER	☐ CANAL
☐ SEA	☐ OCEAN	☐ OTHER

NOTES

Species	Weight	Size	Time

DATE	
TIME	
LOCATION	
COORDINATES	
FISHING PARTNER	

GEAR & EQUIPMENT

FISH BAIT & LURES

WEATHER CONDITIONS

WATER VISIBILITY

1 — 2 — 3 — 4 — 5
CLEAR ... MISTY

MOON PHASE

BODY OF WATER

- [ ] LAKE
- [ ] RIVER
- [ ] CANAL
- [ ] SEA
- [ ] OCEAN
- [ ] OTHER

NOTES

Species	Weight	Size	Time

DATE

TIME

LOCATION

COORDINATES

FISHING PARTNER

GEAR & EQUIPMENT

FISH BAIT & LURES

WEATHER CONDITIONS

WATER VISIBILITY

CLEAR 1 2 3 4 5 MISTY

MOON PHASE

BODY OF WATER

☐ LAKE	☐ RIVER	☐ CANAL
☐ SEA	☐ OCEAN	☐ OTHER

NOTES

Species	Weight	Size	Time

DATE

TIME

LOCATION

COORDINATES

FISHING PARTNER

GEAR & EQUIPMENT

FISH BAIT & LURES

WEATHER CONDITIONS

WATER VISIBILITY

CLEAR 1 2 3 4 5 MISTY

MOON PHASE

BODY OF WATER

☐ LAKE	☐ RIVER	☐ CANAL
☐ SEA	☐ OCEAN	☐ OTHER

NOTES

Species	Weight	Size	Time

DATE

TIME

LOCATION

COORDINATES

FISHING PARTNER

GEAR & EQUIPMENT

FISH BAIT & LURES

WEATHER CONDITIONS

WATER VISIBILITY

CLEAR 1 2 3 4 5 MISTY

MOON PHASE

BODY OF WATER

| LAKE | RIVER | CANAL |
| SEA | OCEAN | OTHER |

NOTES

Species	Weight	Size	Time

DATE	
TIME	
LOCATION	
COORDINATES	
FISHING PARTNER	

GEAR & EQUIPMENT

FISH BAIT & LURES

WEATHER CONDITIONS

WATER VISIBILITY

CLEAR 1 2 3 4 5 MISTY

MOON PHASE

BODY OF WATER

- [ ] LAKE
- [ ] RIVER
- [ ] CANAL
- [ ] SEA
- [ ] OCEAN
- [ ] OTHER

NOTES

Species	Weight	Size	Time

DATE	

TIME	

LOCATION	

COORDINATES	

FISHING PARTNER	

GEAR & EQUIPMENT

FISH BAIT & LURES

WEATHER CONDITIONS

🌡	—	☀	⛅	☁	🌧	❄
🚩	—	☐	☐	☐	☐	☐

WATER VISIBILITY

CLEAR 1 2 3 4 5 MISTY

MOON PHASE

● ● ◐ ☾ ○
☐ ☐ ☐ ☐ ☐

BODY OF WATER

☐ LAKE	☐ RIVER	☐ CANAL
☐ SEA	☐ OCEAN	☐ OTHER

NOTES

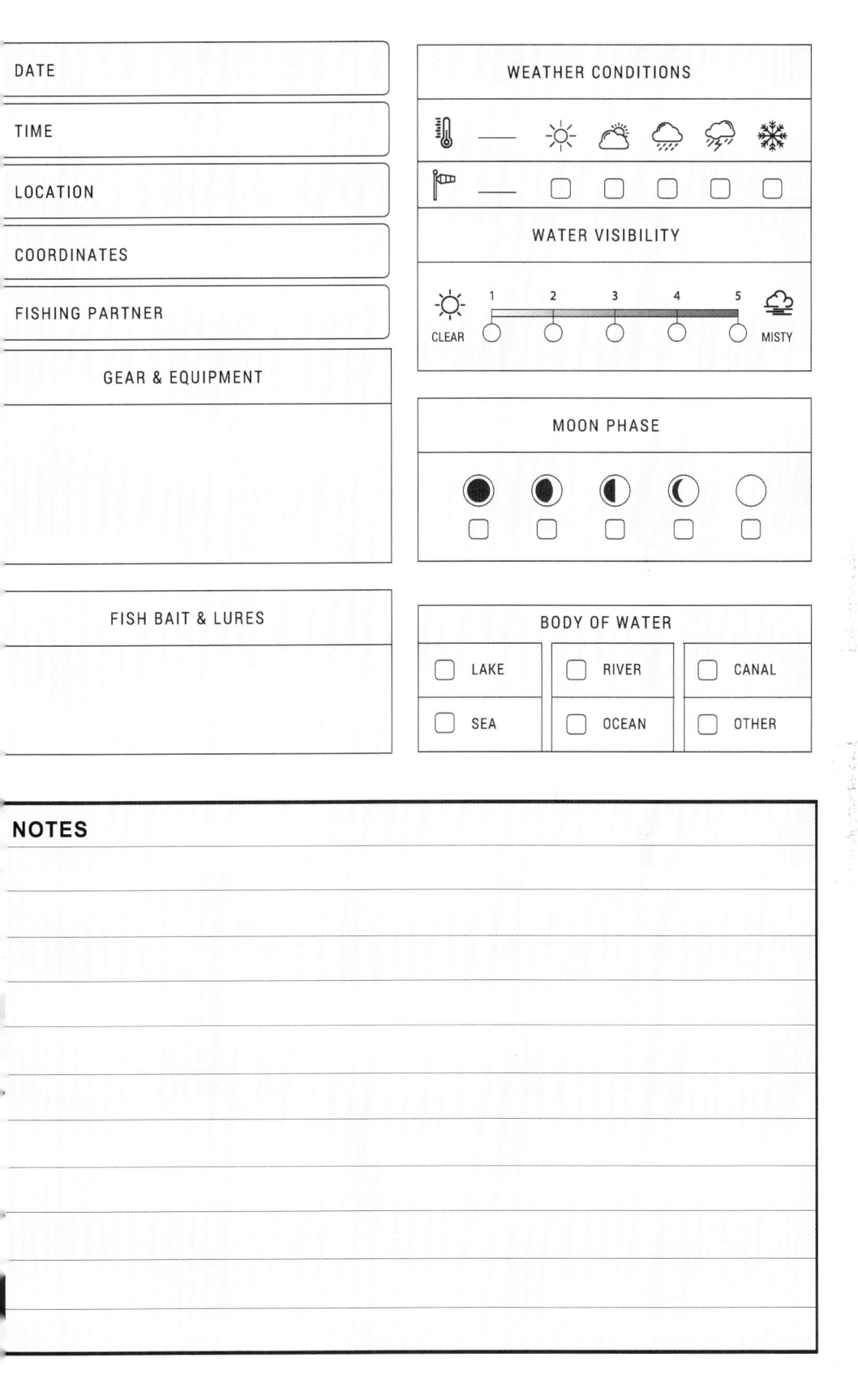

Species	Weight	Size	Time

DATE	
TIME	
LOCATION	
COORDINATES	
FISHING PARTNER	

GEAR & EQUIPMENT

FISH BAIT & LURES

WEATHER CONDITIONS

WATER VISIBILITY

CLEAR 1 2 3 4 5 MISTY

MOON PHASE

BODY OF WATER

- [ ] LAKE
- [ ] RIVER
- [ ] CANAL
- [ ] SEA
- [ ] OCEAN
- [ ] OTHER

NOTES

Species	Weight	Size	Time

DATE

TIME

LOCATION

COORDINATES

FISHING PARTNER

GEAR & EQUIPMENT

FISH BAIT & LURES

WEATHER CONDITIONS

WATER VISIBILITY

CLEAR 1 2 3 4 5 MISTY

MOON PHASE

BODY OF WATER

☐ LAKE	☐ RIVER	☐ CANAL
☐ SEA	☐ OCEAN	☐ OTHER

NOTES

Species	Weight	Size	Time

DATE	
TIME	
LOCATION	
COORDINATES	
FISHING PARTNER	

GEAR & EQUIPMENT

FISH BAIT & LURES

WEATHER CONDITIONS

WATER VISIBILITY

CLEAR 1 2 3 4 5 MISTY

MOON PHASE

BODY OF WATER

☐ LAKE	☐ RIVER	☐ CANAL
☐ SEA	☐ OCEAN	☐ OTHER

NOTES

Species	Weight	Size	Time

DATE	
TIME	
LOCATION	
COORDINATES	
FISHING PARTNER	

GEAR & EQUIPMENT

FISH BAIT & LURES

WEATHER CONDITIONS

WATER VISIBILITY

CLEAR 1 2 3 4 5 MISTY

MOON PHASE

BODY OF WATER

- [ ] LAKE
- [ ] RIVER
- [ ] CANAL
- [ ] SEA
- [ ] OCEAN
- [ ] OTHER

NOTES

Species	Weight	Size	Time

DATE	
TIME	
LOCATION	
COORDINATES	
FISHING PARTNER	

GEAR & EQUIPMENT

FISH BAIT & LURES

WEATHER CONDITIONS

WATER VISIBILITY

CLEAR 1 2 3 4 5 MISTY

MOON PHASE

BODY OF WATER

- [ ] LAKE
- [ ] RIVER
- [ ] CANAL
- [ ] SEA
- [ ] OCEAN
- [ ] OTHER

NOTES

Species	Weight	Size	Time

DATE

TIME

LOCATION

COORDINATES

FISHING PARTNER

GEAR & EQUIPMENT

FISH BAIT & LURES

WEATHER CONDITIONS

WATER VISIBILITY

CLEAR 1 2 3 4 5 MISTY

MOON PHASE

BODY OF WATER

| ☐ LAKE | ☐ RIVER | ☐ CANAL |
| ☐ SEA | ☐ OCEAN | ☐ OTHER |

NOTES

Species	Weight	Size	Time

DATE

TIME

LOCATION

COORDINATES

FISHING PARTNER

GEAR & EQUIPMENT

FISH BAIT & LURES

WEATHER CONDITIONS

WATER VISIBILITY

CLEAR 1 2 3 4 5 MISTY

MOON PHASE

BODY OF WATER

☐ LAKE	☐ RIVER	☐ CANAL
☐ SEA	☐ OCEAN	☐ OTHER

NOTES

Species	Weight	Size	Time

DATE		WEATHER CONDITIONS

TIME

LOCATION

COORDINATES

FISHING PARTNER

GEAR & EQUIPMENT

WATER VISIBILITY

CLEAR 1 2 3 4 5 MISTY

MOON PHASE

FISH BAIT & LURES

BODY OF WATER

- [ ] LAKE
- [ ] RIVER
- [ ] CANAL
- [ ] SEA
- [ ] OCEAN
- [ ] OTHER

NOTES

Species	Weight	Size	Time

DATE	
TIME	
LOCATION	
COORDINATES	
FISHING PARTNER	

GEAR & EQUIPMENT

FISH BAIT & LURES

WEATHER CONDITIONS

WATER VISIBILITY

CLEAR 1 — 2 — 3 — 4 — 5 MISTY

MOON PHASE

BODY OF WATER

- [ ] LAKE
- [ ] RIVER
- [ ] CANAL
- [ ] SEA
- [ ] OCEAN
- [ ] OTHER

NOTES

Species	Weight	Size	Time

DATE	

TIME	

LOCATION	

COORDINATES	

FISHING PARTNER	

GEAR & EQUIPMENT

FISH BAIT & LURES

WEATHER CONDITIONS

WATER VISIBILITY

CLEAR 1 2 3 4 5 MISTY

MOON PHASE

BODY OF WATER

- ☐ LAKE
- ☐ RIVER
- ☐ CANAL
- ☐ SEA
- ☐ OCEAN
- ☐ OTHER

NOTES

Species	Weight	Size	Time

DATE		WEATHER CONDITIONS

TIME

LOCATION

COORDINATES

FISHING PARTNER

GEAR & EQUIPMENT

FISH BAIT & LURES

WATER VISIBILITY

1 — CLEAR 2 3 4 5 — MISTY

MOON PHASE

BODY OF WATER

- ☐ LAKE
- ☐ SEA
- ☐ RIVER
- ☐ OCEAN
- ☐ CANAL
- ☐ OTHER

NOTES

Species	Weight	Size	Time

DATE

TIME

LOCATION

COORDINATES

FISHING PARTNER

GEAR & EQUIPMENT

FISH BAIT & LURES

WEATHER CONDITIONS

WATER VISIBILITY

CLEAR 1 2 3 4 5 MISTY

MOON PHASE

BODY OF WATER

- [ ] LAKE
- [ ] RIVER
- [ ] CANAL
- [ ] SEA
- [ ] OCEAN
- [ ] OTHER

NOTES

Species	Weight	Size	Time

DATE	WEATHER CONDITIONS

TIME

LOCATION

COORDINATES

WATER VISIBILITY

1   2   3   4   5

CLEAR   MISTY

FISHING PARTNER

GEAR & EQUIPMENT

MOON PHASE

FISH BAIT & LURES

BODY OF WATER

- [ ] LAKE
- [ ] RIVER
- [ ] CANAL
- [ ] SEA
- [ ] OCEAN
- [ ] OTHER

NOTES

Species	Weight	Size	Time

DATE	
TIME	
LOCATION	
COORDINATES	
FISHING PARTNER	

GEAR & EQUIPMENT

FISH BAIT & LURES

WEATHER CONDITIONS

WATER VISIBILITY
CLEAR 1 2 3 4 5 MISTY

MOON PHASE

BODY OF WATER
- [ ] LAKE
- [ ] RIVER
- [ ] CANAL
- [ ] SEA
- [ ] OCEAN
- [ ] OTHER

NOTES

Species	Weight	Size	Time

DATE

TIME

LOCATION

COORDINATES

FISHING PARTNER

GEAR & EQUIPMENT

FISH BAIT & LURES

WEATHER CONDITIONS

WATER VISIBILITY

CLEAR 1 2 3 4 5 MISTY

MOON PHASE

BODY OF WATER

- [ ] LAKE
- [ ] RIVER
- [ ] CANAL
- [ ] SEA
- [ ] OCEAN
- [ ] OTHER

NOTES

Species	Weight	Size	Time

DATE

TIME

LOCATION

COORDINATES

FISHING PARTNER

GEAR & EQUIPMENT

FISH BAIT & LURES

WEATHER CONDITIONS

WATER VISIBILITY

CLEAR 1 2 3 4 5 MISTY

MOON PHASE

BODY OF WATER

☐ LAKE	☐ RIVER	☐ CANAL
☐ SEA	☐ OCEAN	☐ OTHER

NOTES

Species	Weight	Size	Time

DATE	
TIME	
LOCATION	
COORDINATES	
FISHING PARTNER	

GEAR & EQUIPMENT

FISH BAIT & LURES

WEATHER CONDITIONS

WATER VISIBILITY

CLEAR 1 2 3 4 5 MISTY

MOON PHASE

BODY OF WATER

- [ ] LAKE
- [ ] RIVER
- [ ] CANAL
- [ ] SEA
- [ ] OCEAN
- [ ] OTHER

NOTES

Species	Weight	Size	Time

DATE	
TIME	
LOCATION	
COORDINATES	
FISHING PARTNER	

GEAR & EQUIPMENT

WEATHER CONDITIONS

WATER VISIBILITY

1 — 2 — 3 — 4 — 5
CLEAR → MISTY

MOON PHASE

FISH BAIT & LURES

BODY OF WATER

- ☐ LAKE
- ☐ RIVER
- ☐ CANAL
- ☐ SEA
- ☐ OCEAN
- ☐ OTHER

NOTES

Species	Weight	Size	Time

DATE

TIME

LOCATION

COORDINATES

FISHING PARTNER

GEAR & EQUIPMENT

FISH BAIT & LURES

WEATHER CONDITIONS

WATER VISIBILITY

| CLEAR | 1 | 2 | 3 | 4 | 5 | MISTY |

MOON PHASE

BODY OF WATER

| ☐ LAKE | ☐ RIVER | ☐ CANAL |
| ☐ SEA | ☐ OCEAN | ☐ OTHER |

NOTES

Species	Weight	Size	Time

DATE	
TIME	
LOCATION	
COORDINATES	
FISHING PARTNER	

GEAR & EQUIPMENT

FISH BAIT & LURES

WEATHER CONDITIONS

WATER VISIBILITY

CLEAR 1 2 3 4 5 MISTY

MOON PHASE

BODY OF WATER

- [ ] LAKE
- [ ] RIVER
- [ ] CANAL
- [ ] SEA
- [ ] OCEAN
- [ ] OTHER

NOTES

Species	Weight	Size	Time

DATE	WEATHER CONDITIONS

TIME

LOCATION

COORDINATES

FISHING PARTNER

GEAR & EQUIPMENT

WATER VISIBILITY

CLEAR 1 2 3 4 5 MISTY

MOON PHASE

FISH BAIT & LURES

BODY OF WATER

- [ ] LAKE
- [ ] RIVER
- [ ] CANAL
- [ ] SEA
- [ ] OCEAN
- [ ] OTHER

NOTES

Species	Weight	Size	Time

DATE

TIME

LOCATION

COORDINATES

FISHING PARTNER

GEAR & EQUIPMENT

FISH BAIT & LURES

WEATHER CONDITIONS

WATER VISIBILITY

CLEAR 1 2 3 4 5 MISTY

MOON PHASE

BODY OF WATER

- [ ] LAKE
- [ ] RIVER
- [ ] CANAL
- [ ] SEA
- [ ] OCEAN
- [ ] OTHER

NOTES

Species	Weight	Size	Time

DATE	

TIME	

LOCATION	

COORDINATES	

FISHING PARTNER	

GEAR & EQUIPMENT

FISH BAIT & LURES

WEATHER CONDITIONS

WATER VISIBILITY

CLEAR 1 2 3 4 5 MISTY

MOON PHASE

BODY OF WATER

- [ ] LAKE
- [ ] RIVER
- [ ] CANAL
- [ ] SEA
- [ ] OCEAN
- [ ] OTHER

NOTES

Species	Weight	Size	Time

DATE

TIME

LOCATION

COORDINATES

FISHING PARTNER

GEAR & EQUIPMENT

FISH BAIT & LURES

WEATHER CONDITIONS

WATER VISIBILITY

CLEAR 1 2 3 4 5 MISTY

MOON PHASE

BODY OF WATER

- [ ] LAKE
- [ ] RIVER
- [ ] CANAL
- [ ] SEA
- [ ] OCEAN
- [ ] OTHER

NOTES

Species	Weight	Size	Time

DATE

TIME

LOCATION

COORDINATES

FISHING PARTNER

GEAR & EQUIPMENT

FISH BAIT & LURES

WEATHER CONDITIONS

WATER VISIBILITY

1	2	3	4	5
CLEAR — MISTY

MOON PHASE

BODY OF WATER

- [ ] LAKE
- [ ] RIVER
- [ ] CANAL
- [ ] SEA
- [ ] OCEAN
- [ ] OTHER

NOTES

Species	Weight	Size	Time

DATE

TIME

LOCATION

COORDINATES

FISHING PARTNER

GEAR & EQUIPMENT

FISH BAIT & LURES

WEATHER CONDITIONS

WATER VISIBILITY

CLEAR 1 2 3 4 5 MISTY

MOON PHASE

BODY OF WATER

- [ ] LAKE
- [ ] RIVER
- [ ] CANAL
- [ ] SEA
- [ ] OCEAN
- [ ] OTHER

NOTES

Species	Weight	Size	Time

DATE

TIME

LOCATION

COORDINATES

FISHING PARTNER

GEAR & EQUIPMENT

FISH BAIT & LURES

WEATHER CONDITIONS

WATER VISIBILITY

1	2	3	4	5
CLEAR — MISTY

MOON PHASE

BODY OF WATER

| ☐ LAKE | ☐ RIVER | ☐ CANAL |
| ☐ SEA | ☐ OCEAN | ☐ OTHER |

NOTES

Species	Weight	Size	Time

DATE

TIME

LOCATION

COORDINATES

FISHING PARTNER

GEAR & EQUIPMENT

FISH BAIT & LURES

WEATHER CONDITIONS

WATER VISIBILITY

CLEAR 1 2 3 4 5 MISTY

MOON PHASE

BODY OF WATER

☐ LAKE	☐ RIVER	☐ CANAL
☐ SEA	☐ OCEAN	☐ OTHER

NOTES

Species	Weight	Size	Time

DATE	WEATHER CONDITIONS

TIME	

LOCATION	

WATER VISIBILITY

COORDINATES	

	1	2	3	4	5	
CLEAR	○	○	○	○	○	MISTY

FISHING PARTNER

GEAR & EQUIPMENT

MOON PHASE

FISH BAIT & LURES

BODY OF WATER

☐ LAKE	☐ RIVER	☐ CANAL
☐ SEA	☐ OCEAN	☐ OTHER

NOTES

Species	Weight	Size	Time

DATE	
TIME	
LOCATION	
COORDINATES	
FISHING PARTNER	

GEAR & EQUIPMENT

FISH BAIT & LURES

WEATHER CONDITIONS

WATER VISIBILITY

CLEAR 1 2 3 4 5 MISTY

MOON PHASE

BODY OF WATER

☐ LAKE	☐ RIVER	☐ CANAL
☐ SEA	☐ OCEAN	☐ OTHER

NOTES

Species	Weight	Size	Time

DATE

TIME

LOCATION

COORDINATES

FISHING PARTNER

GEAR & EQUIPMENT

FISH BAIT & LURES

WEATHER CONDITIONS

WATER VISIBILITY

1　2　3　4　5
CLEAR　　　　　　　　　　MISTY

MOON PHASE

BODY OF WATER

| ☐ LAKE | ☐ RIVER | ☐ CANAL |
| ☐ SEA | ☐ OCEAN | ☐ OTHER |

NOTES

Species	Weight	Size	Time

DATE

TIME

LOCATION

COORDINATES

FISHING PARTNER

GEAR & EQUIPMENT

FISH BAIT & LURES

WEATHER CONDITIONS

WATER VISIBILITY

| 1 | 2 | 3 | 4 | 5 |
CLEAR — MISTY

MOON PHASE

BODY OF WATER

- [ ] LAKE
- [ ] RIVER
- [ ] CANAL
- [ ] SEA
- [ ] OCEAN
- [ ] OTHER

NOTES

Species	Weight	Size	Time

DATE

TIME

LOCATION

COORDINATES

FISHING PARTNER

GEAR & EQUIPMENT

FISH BAIT & LURES

WEATHER CONDITIONS

WATER VISIBILITY

CLEAR 1 2 3 4 5 MISTY

MOON PHASE

BODY OF WATER

☐ LAKE	☐ RIVER	☐ CANAL
☐ SEA	☐ OCEAN	☐ OTHER

NOTES

Species	Weight	Size	Time

DATE	
TIME	
LOCATION	
COORDINATES	
FISHING PARTNER	

GEAR & EQUIPMENT

FISH BAIT & LURES

WEATHER CONDITIONS

WATER VISIBILITY

CLEAR 1 2 3 4 5 MISTY

MOON PHASE

BODY OF WATER

- ☐ LAKE
- ☐ SEA
- ☐ RIVER
- ☐ OCEAN
- ☐ CANAL
- ☐ OTHER

NOTES

Species	Weight	Size	Time

DATE	
TIME	
LOCATION	
COORDINATES	
FISHING PARTNER	

GEAR & EQUIPMENT

FISH BAIT & LURES

WEATHER CONDITIONS

WATER VISIBILITY

CLEAR 1 2 3 4 5 MISTY

MOON PHASE

BODY OF WATER

- [ ] LAKE
- [ ] RIVER
- [ ] CANAL
- [ ] SEA
- [ ] OCEAN
- [ ] OTHER

NOTES

Species	Weight	Size	Time

DATE

TIME

LOCATION

COORDINATES

FISHING PARTNER

GEAR & EQUIPMENT

FISH BAIT & LURES

WEATHER CONDITIONS

WATER VISIBILITY

CLEAR 1 2 3 4 5 MISTY

MOON PHASE

BODY OF WATER

- [ ] LAKE
- [ ] RIVER
- [ ] CANAL
- [ ] SEA
- [ ] OCEAN
- [ ] OTHER

NOTES

Printed in Great Britain
by Amazon